# THE CLASH WITHIN

# The Clash Within

DEMOCRACY,

RELIGIOUS VIOLENCE,

AND

INDIA'S FUTURE

*Martha C. Nussbaum*

The Belknap Press of
Harvard University Press

*Cambridge, Massachusetts*
*London, England*

First Harvard University Press paperback edition, 2008.

*Library of Congress Cataloging-in-Publication Data*

Nussbaum, Martha Craven, 1947–
The clash within : democracy, religious violence, and India's future /
Martha C. Nussbaum.
p.   cm.
Includes bibliographical references and index.
ISBN 978-0-674-02482-3 (cloth : alk. paper)
ISBN 978-0-674-03059-6 (pbk.)
1. Hindutva.   2. Communalism—India.   3. Hinduism and state.   4. Violence—
Religious aspects—Hinduism.   5. Democracy—India.   6. Religious fanaticism—
Hinduism.   I. Title.

DS422.C64N88 2007      2006049715

*FOR AMITA SEN*